TATYANA MURRAY

In the Woods

BOSI CONTEMPORARY
May 5 – June 2

Front cover: *Snakes and Ladders,* 2013 (detail)
Design: Vittorio Calabrese
Text editing: Kara Brooks
Photo by Etienne Frossard (◆)

ISBN: 978-1-300-96369-1

CONTENTS

Tatyana Murray's work explores afflictions of the human condition: mortality, isolation, conflict, the compulsion to harness and control nature, loss of innocence, and the role of authority. Though the artwork addresses these darker facets, Murray has chosen light as a constant theme, as it illustrates the fragility and ever changing aspect of life. Murray works with mixed-media sculptures, drawings, and etched light boxes to create themes of skulls, animal physiognomic, ghost trees and young schoolgirls in trance like states. Being a self-taught artist, imagination and intuition play a significant role in the development of Murray's artistic vision.

Her etched light boxes use high-end technology — programmed LED light — with classical drawing techniques. Scratch marks are etched and sculpted into the multiple layers of glass. Once turned on, the light source refracts off the markings, creating the illusion of movement and three-dimensionality. This generates a tension between the old and the new, ultimately addressing the issue of time. Through the violent act of scratching onto glass, the refracted light reveals a delicate portrait but, once the light is off, the image disappears. The eye passes through the layers of glass the way memory passes through time. The figures are suspended within the clear block, creating a fragile tension between the solid and the ethereal, the traditional and the experimental, nostalgia and utopia.

Murray's light box images of young schoolgirls are inspired by her childhood memories spent in British boarding schools. In this series titled *Dystopia*, she portrays cloned girls, all dressed in identical school uniforms, occupying a lawless world. These schoolgirls, almost in a trance like state, are staged in a primordial forest Consumed with dark romantic scenarios of pagan rituals, sacrifices and exorcisms., they hover between a fantastical world full of wonderment, and the disintegration of order ruled by dark forces. The girls are in the stage of early childhood, 3 to 5 years old, a time of self-discovery, realizing their physical strength and the desire to belong but yet be autonomous.

The *Ghost Trees* and *Skulls* etchings invite the viewer to meditate on the fleetingness of nature and life, ultimately to suspend the inevitable, immanent arrival of death. On the reverse the images are also a celebration of nature and man. As a child, Murray would play amongst the apple trees in the field behind her house. The twisting branches and undulating trunks made an indelible impression on her, which carried over as her inspiration for this series. She decided to use trees as the main subject of this series, not only because of their symbolism, but also to address the sense of loss she experienced when returning to her childhood home a few years ago a housing complex had replaced all the trees. In the case of this series, when our eye passes through the etched light boxes' transparent layers, so our senses can travel back to when these ghost trees lived. They are delicate hauntings, not clamoring protests, loyalists to beauty against the forces of indiscriminate destruction.

Growing up, the artist made sense of the world through fairy tales and imagination. She studied *Lord of the Flies* and the Grimm's Fairy Tales were read to her by her mother. Murray found these stories both terrifying and intriguing. Her artwork at times is autobiographical, but the impact is universal; good versus evil, handling infancy and memory in its fantastical dimension shared by everyone. She places the viewer in an intermediate world between dream and wakefulness, between a child's nightmare and Fairy Tale.

EXHIBITED WORKS

LIGHT BOXES

GHOST TREE #25
2010
LED lights, glass, plexiglass, wood
62 x 24 x 12 in.

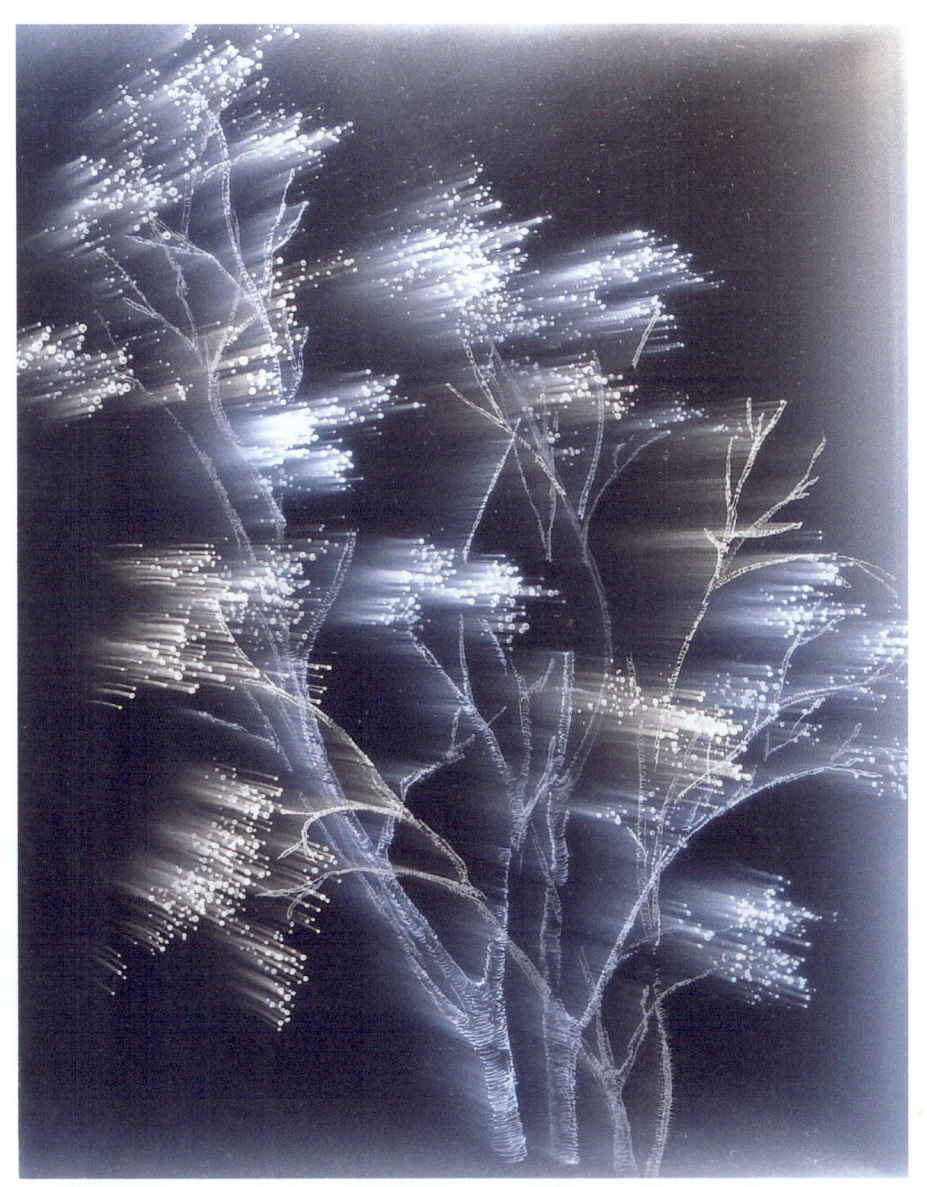

GHOST TREE #26
2010
LED lights, glass, plexiglass, wood
87 x 32 x 18 in.

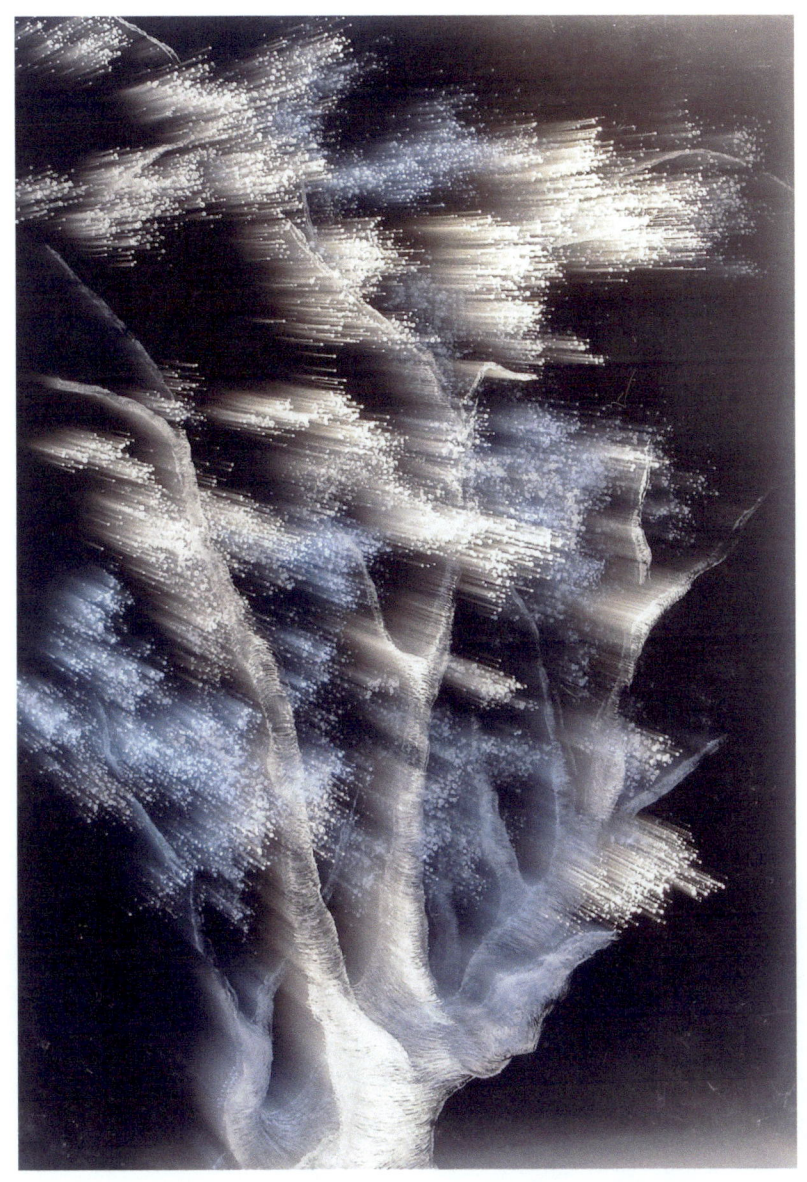

GHOST TREE #31
2010
LED lights, glass, plexiglass, wood
82 x 32 x 17 in.

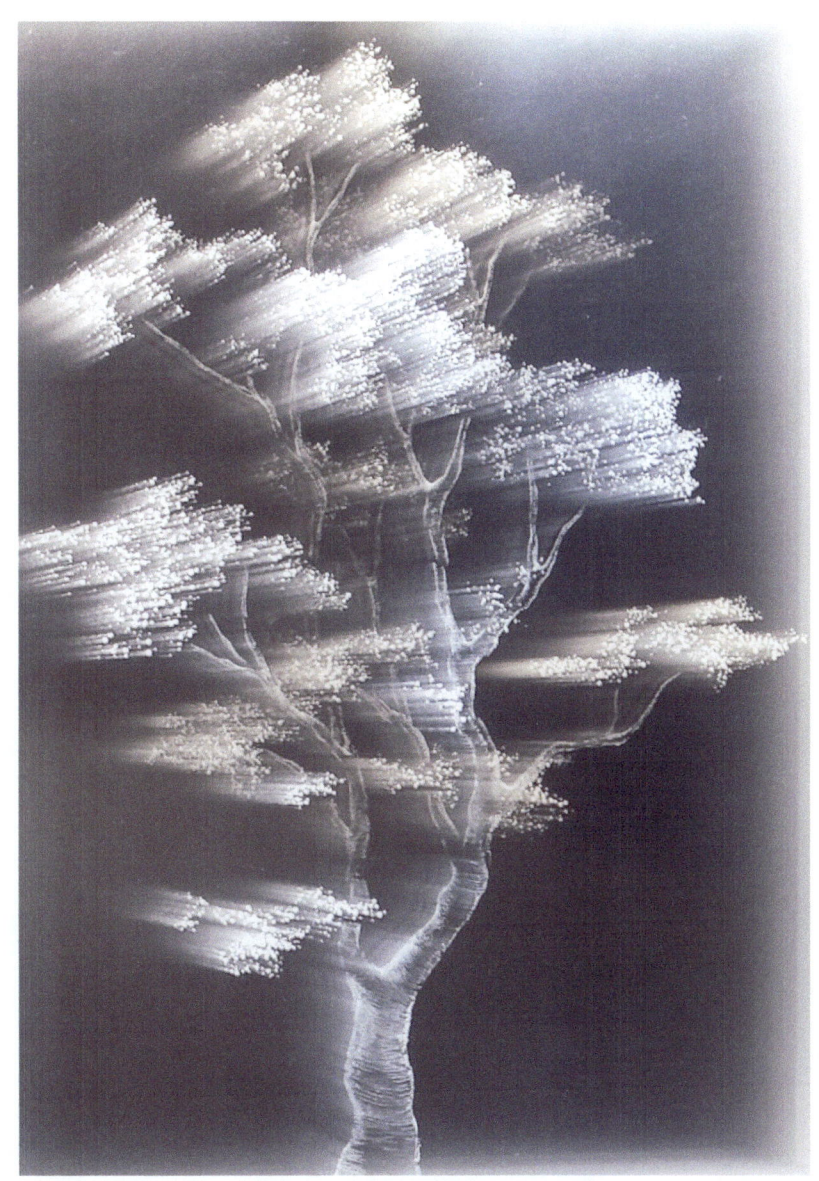

SNAKES AND LADDERS
2013
LED lights, glass, plexiglass, wood
23 x 29 x 5½ in.

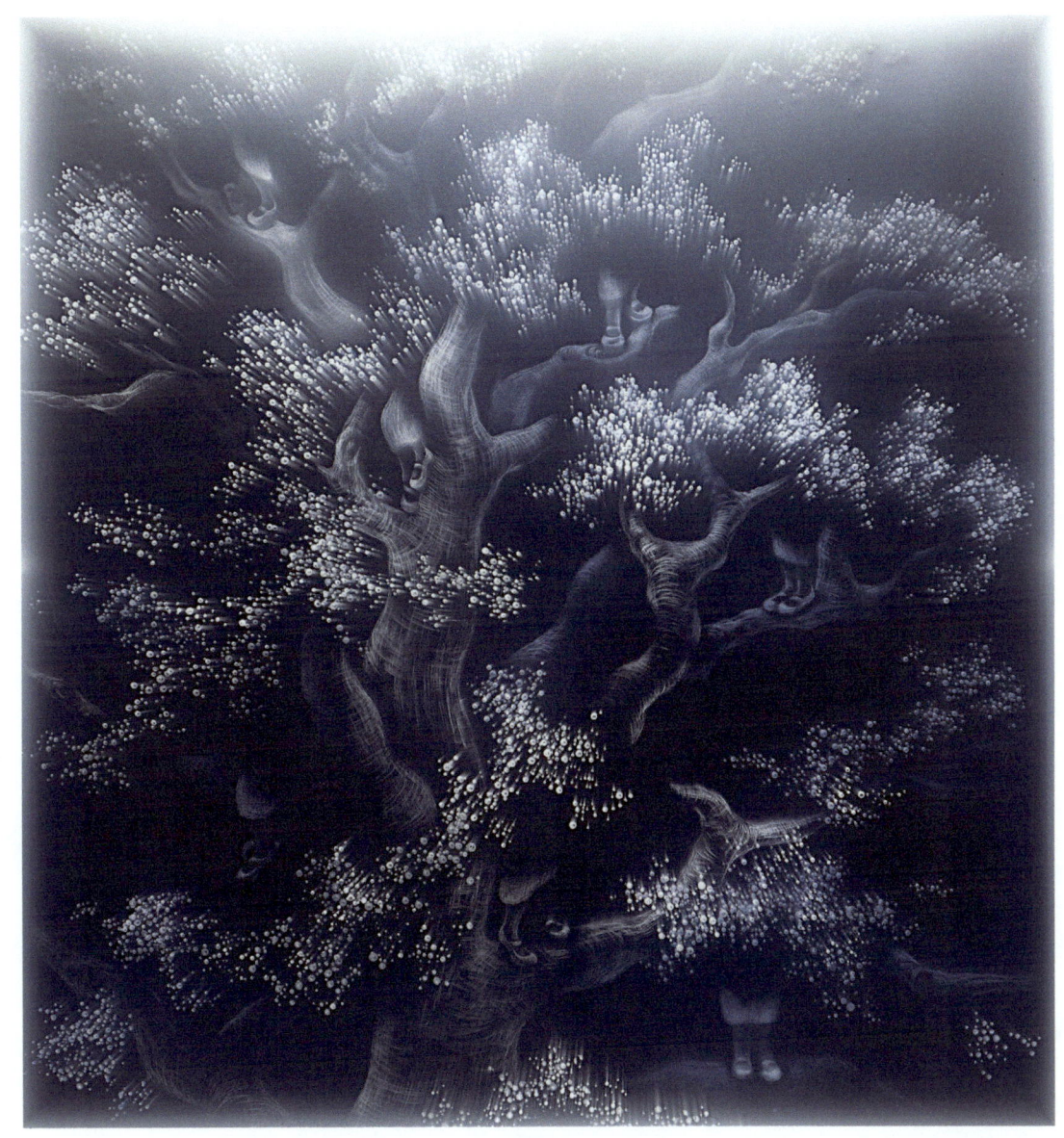

SNAKES AND LADDERS 2 ◆
2013
LED lights, glass, plexiglass, wood
48 x 31 x 6 in.

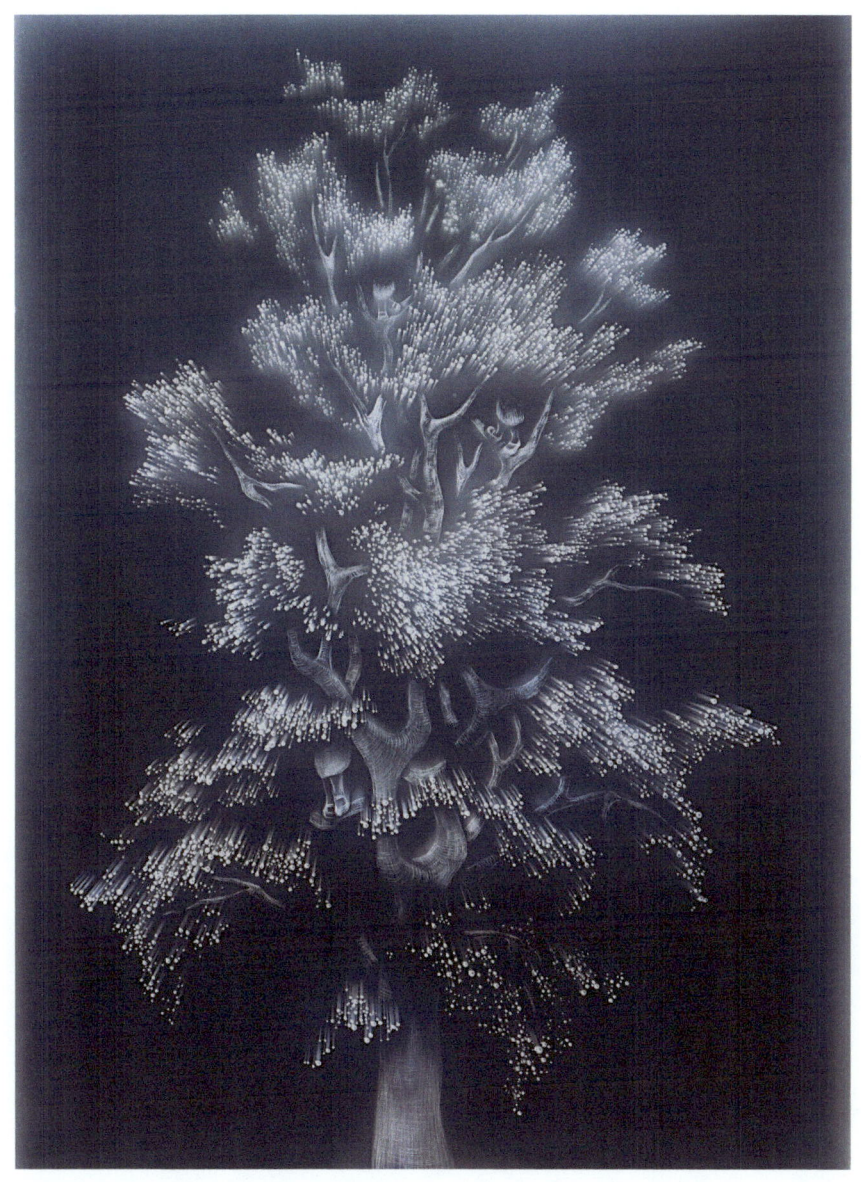

BELLA
2012
LED lights, glass, plexiglass, wood
26 x 19 x 5 in.

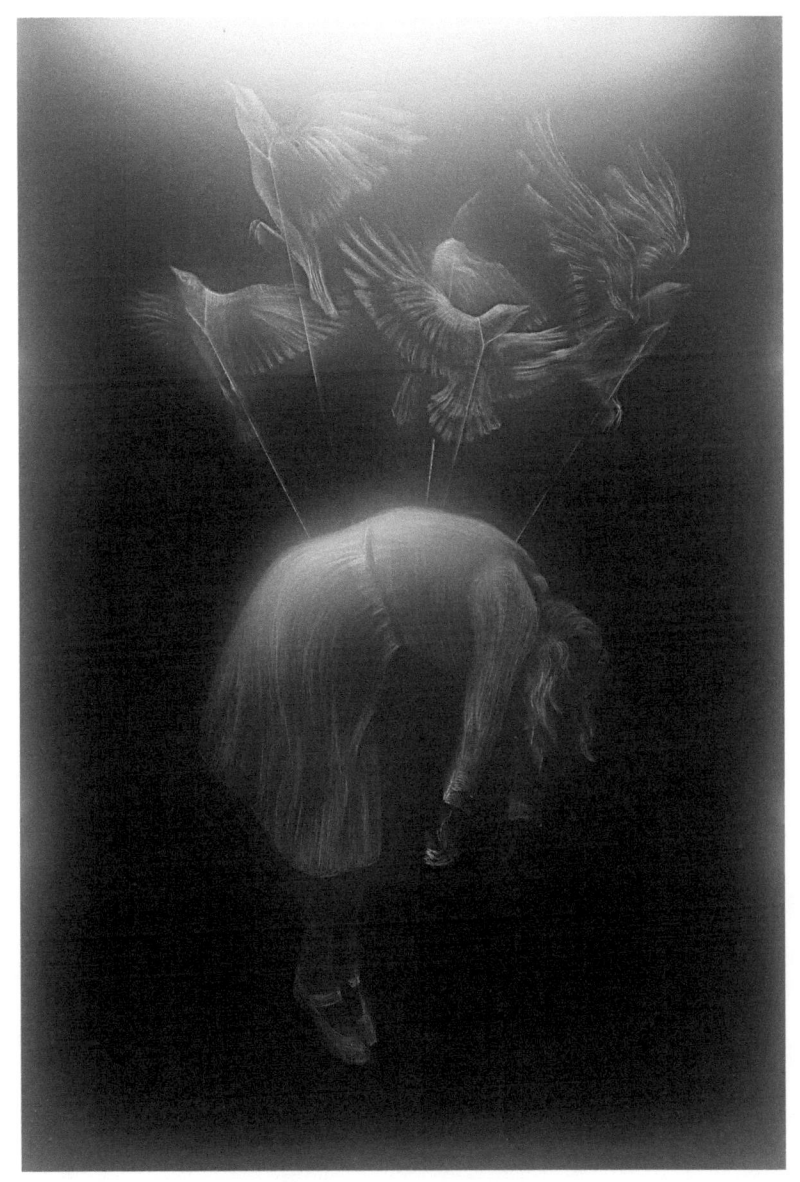

STELLA
2012
LED lights, glass, plexiglass, wood
42 x 22 x 5¼ in.

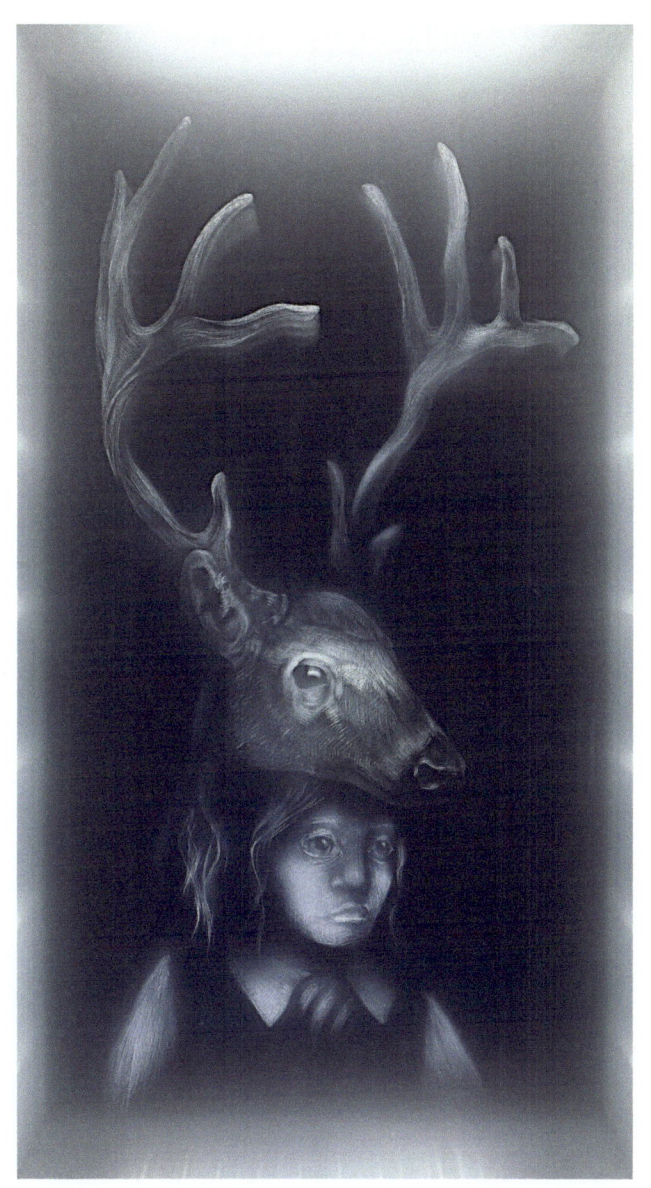

ANNA
2012
LED lights, glass, plexiglass, wood
36 x 23 x 5¼ in.

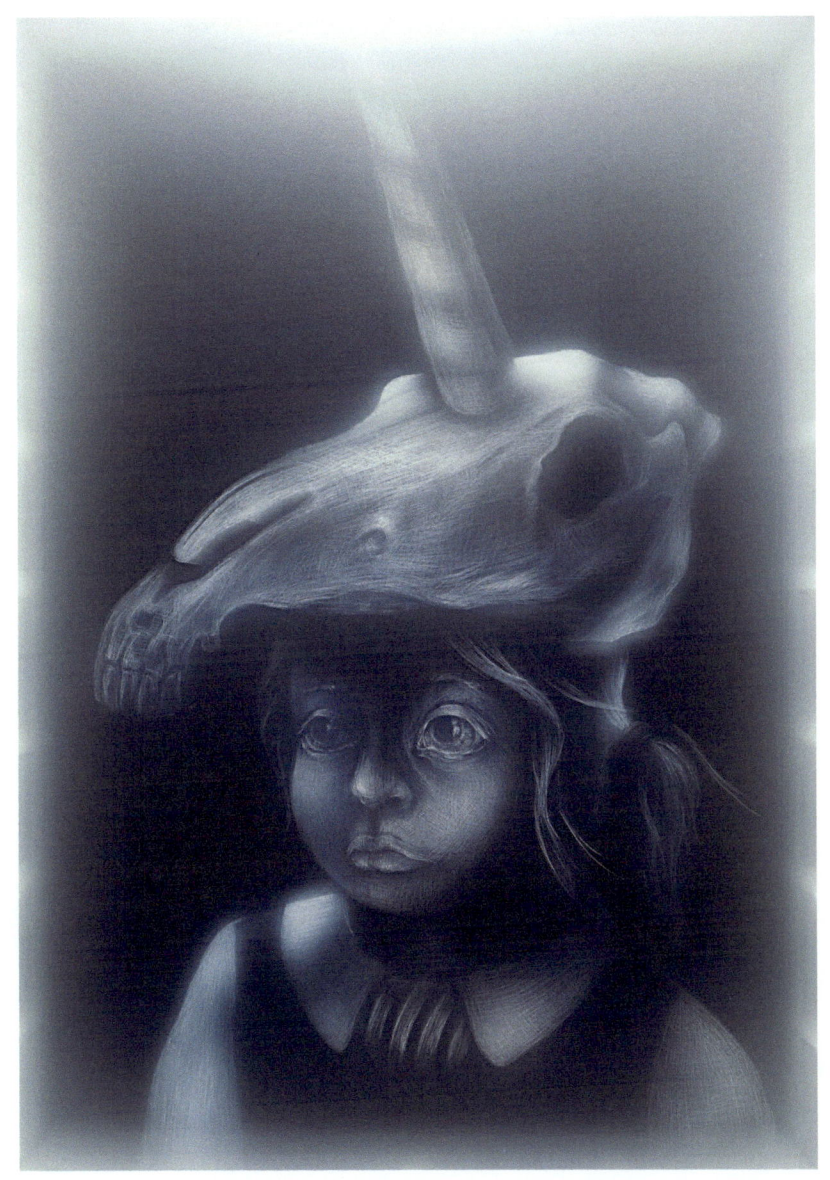

SKULL
2011
LED lights, glass, plexiglass, wood
51 x 32 x 5 in.

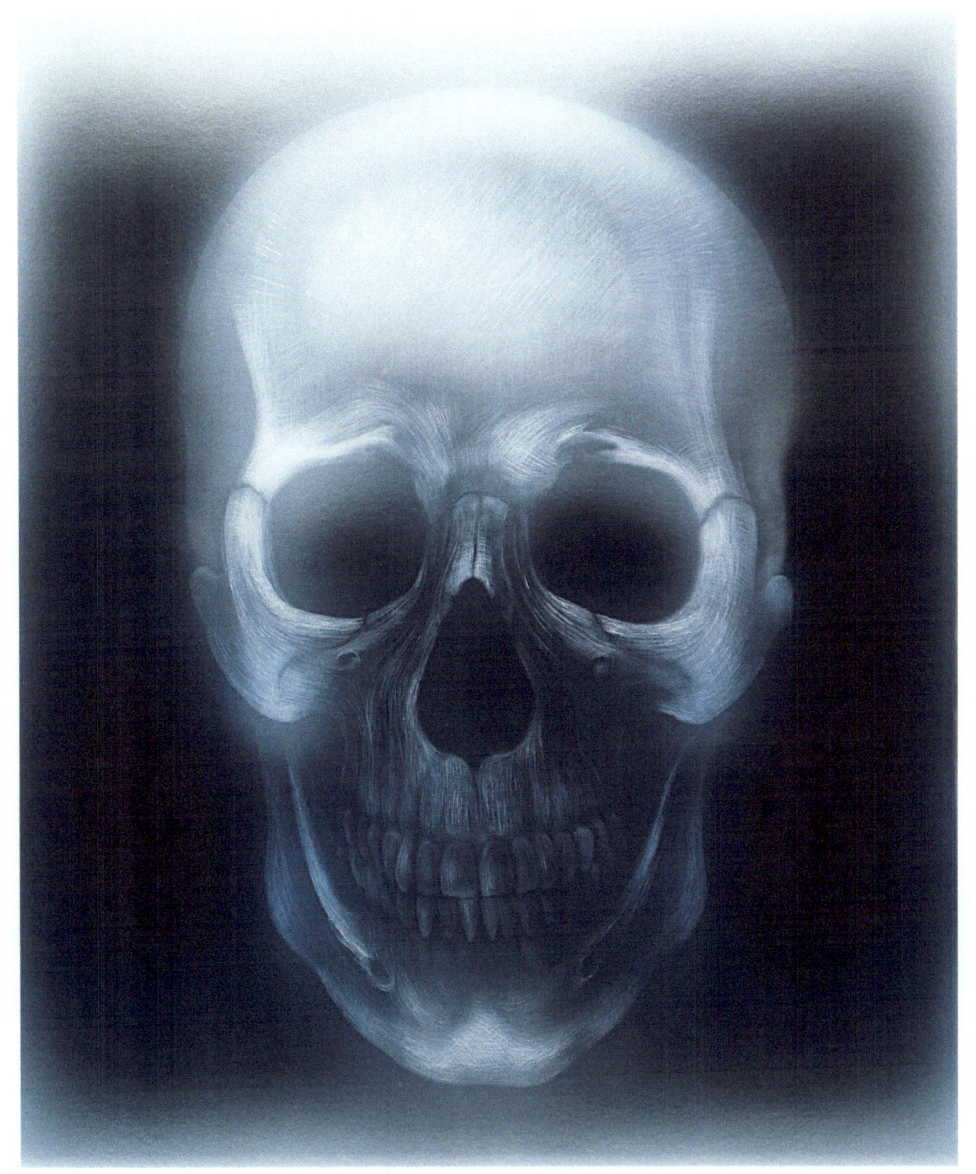

KING OF THE FOREST
2012
LED lights, glass, plexiglass, wood
60 x 38 x 5¼ in.

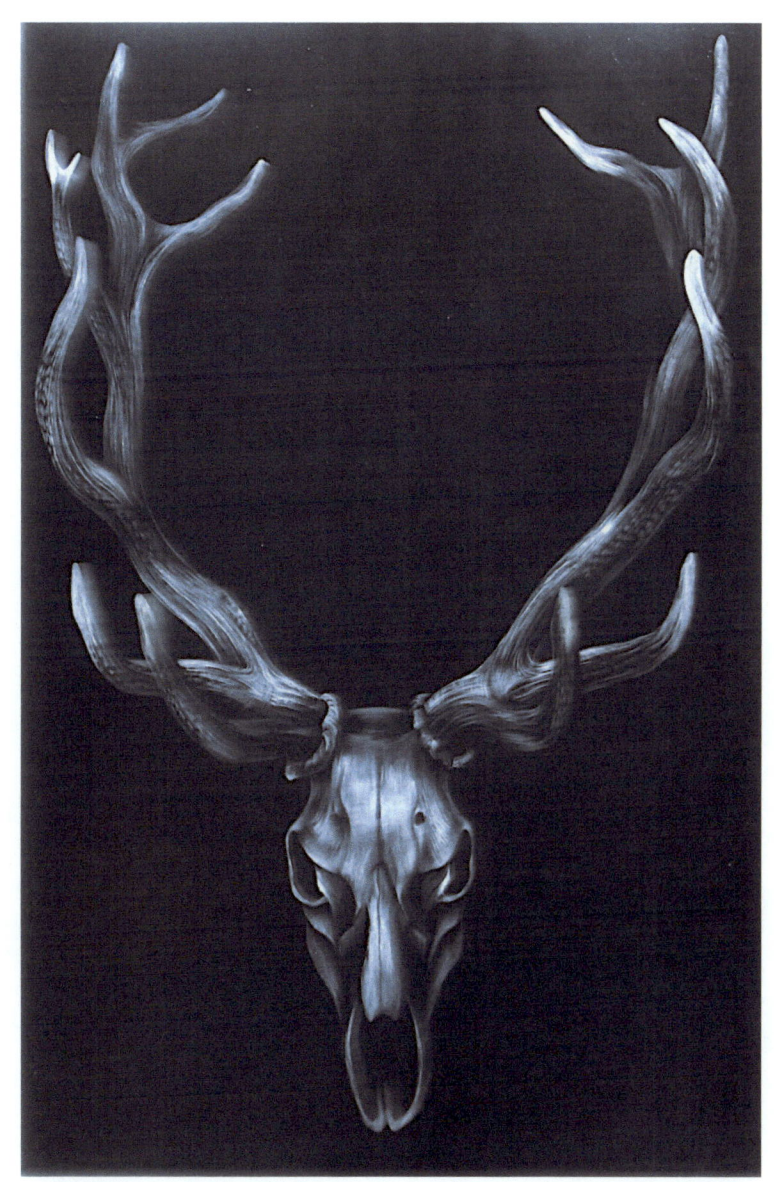

Drawing has been a pivotal part of Murray's work. Though the drawings appear sparse and elemental, they come out of hundreds of sketched ideas, concepts and visions. With the intention to make a flat, two-dimension image, three dimensionally translated in the work, she uses overlapping layers of vellum paper — some different sizes from the other.

The translucency of the paper creates different intensities of ochre with the straight perpendicular edges, creating a grid formation. The different layers give a sense of depth and the grid like formations from the papers' edge can be seen as a subconscious structure imposed on the scenes, unfolding between the girls and animals.

Murray invites the viewer to contemplate the question of what authority is, what is the outside force commanding these girls in identical uniforms, and whether it is the girls dominating the animals or vice versa.

THE HUNT
2013
velum, tape, paint, pencil, charcoal
42 x 25 in.

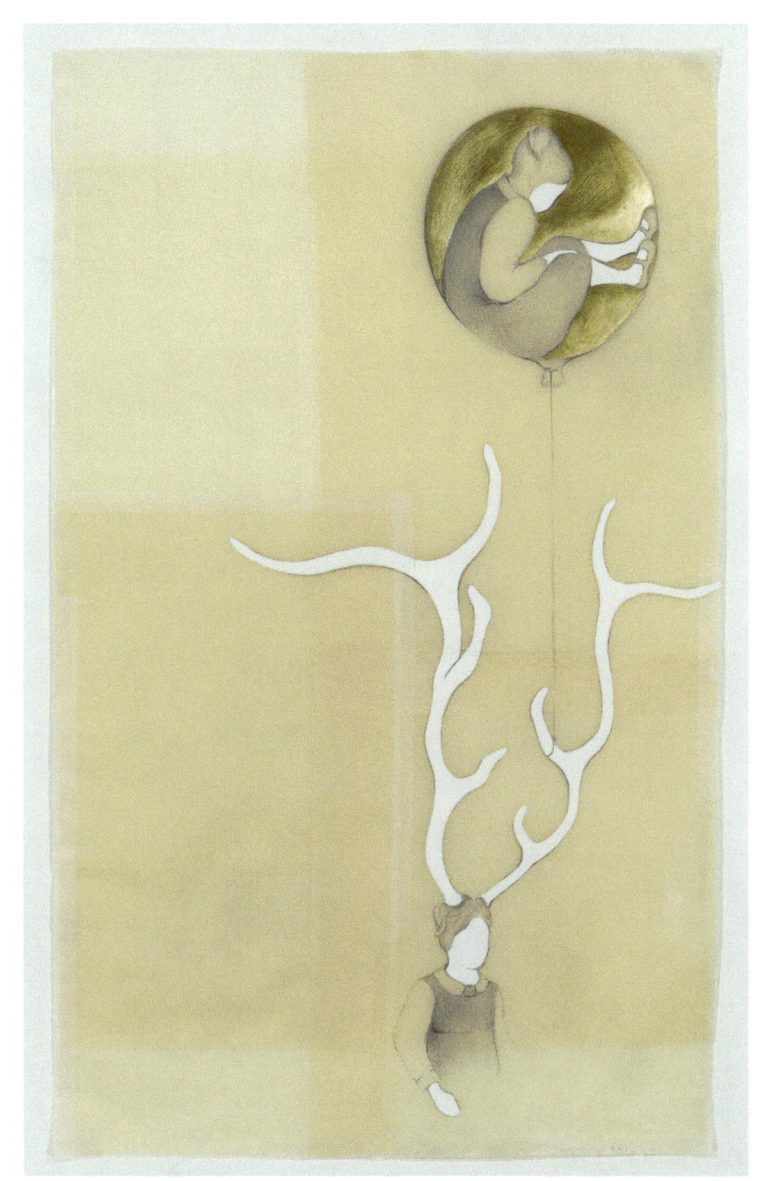

CONTEMPLATION ◆
2013
velum, tape, paint, pencil, charcoal
38 x 25 in.

34

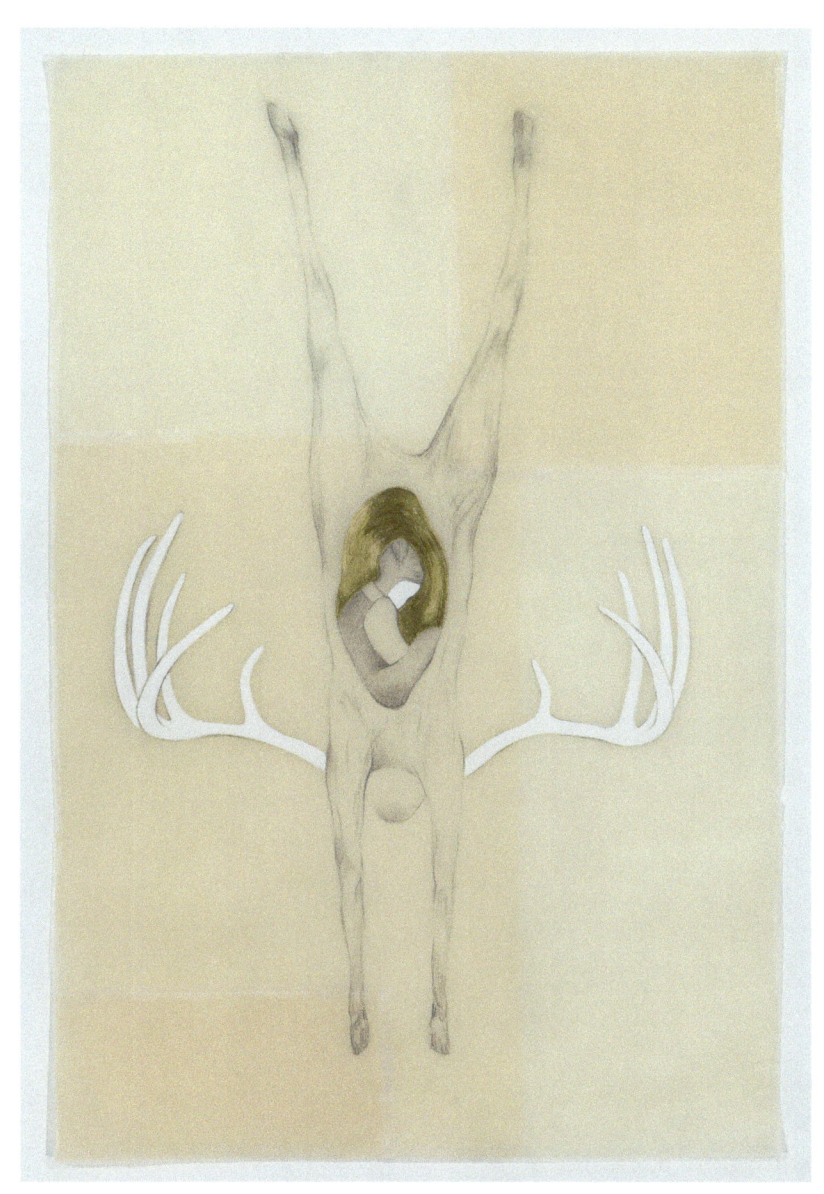

JUDGMENT ◆
2013
velum, tape, paint, pencil, charcoal
25 x 38 in.

36

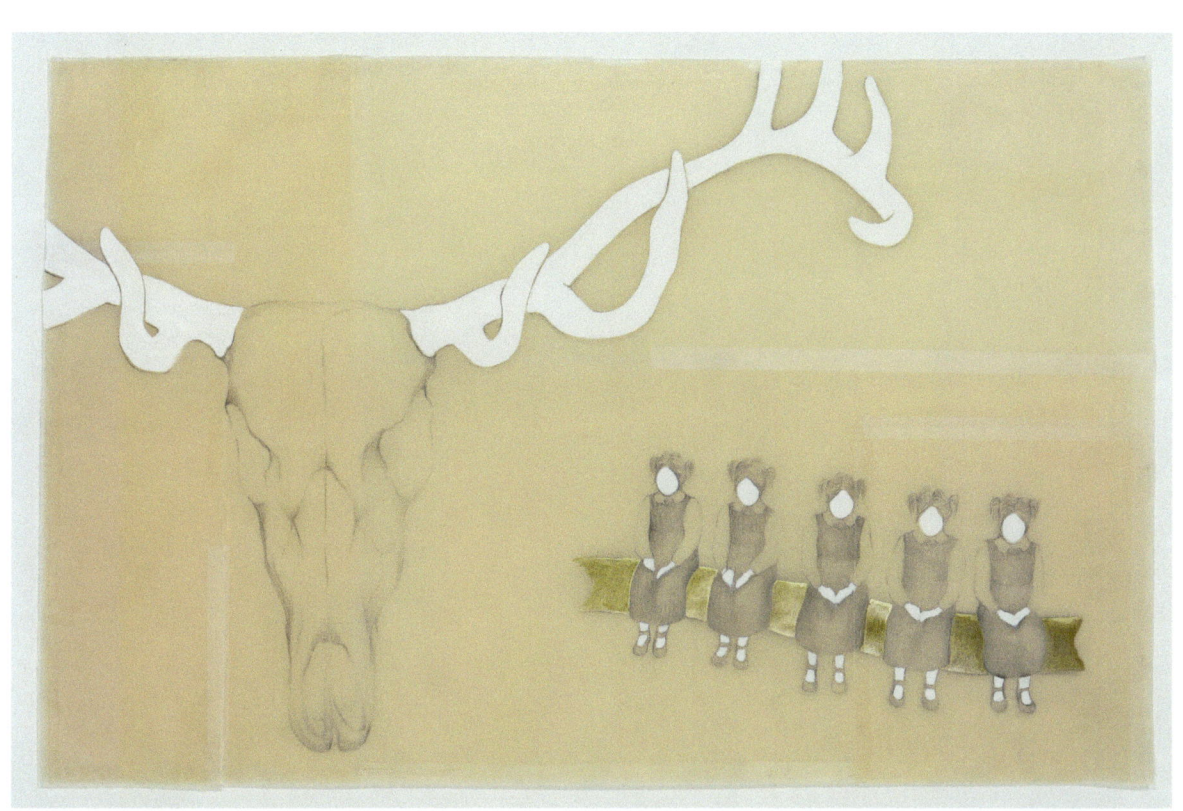

THE RUNAROUND ◆
2013
velum, tape, paint, pencil, charcoal
41 x 24 in.

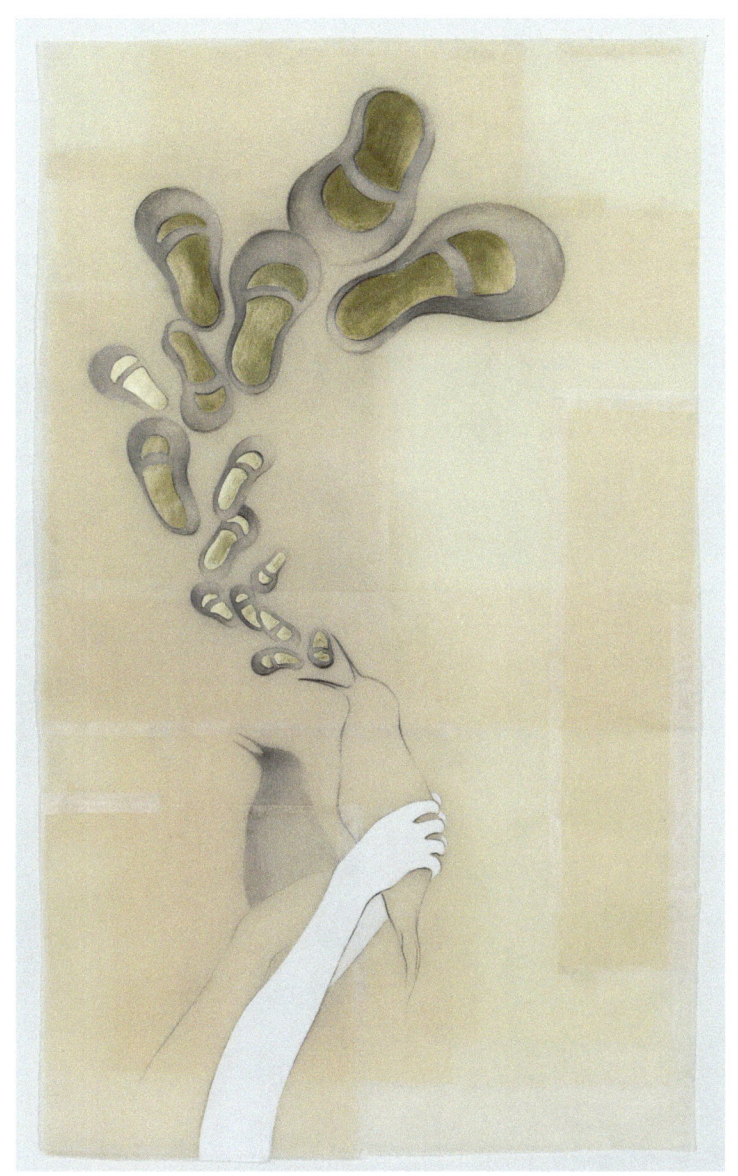

ENTRAPMENT ◆
2013
velum, tape, paint, pencil, charcoal
31½ x 38 in.

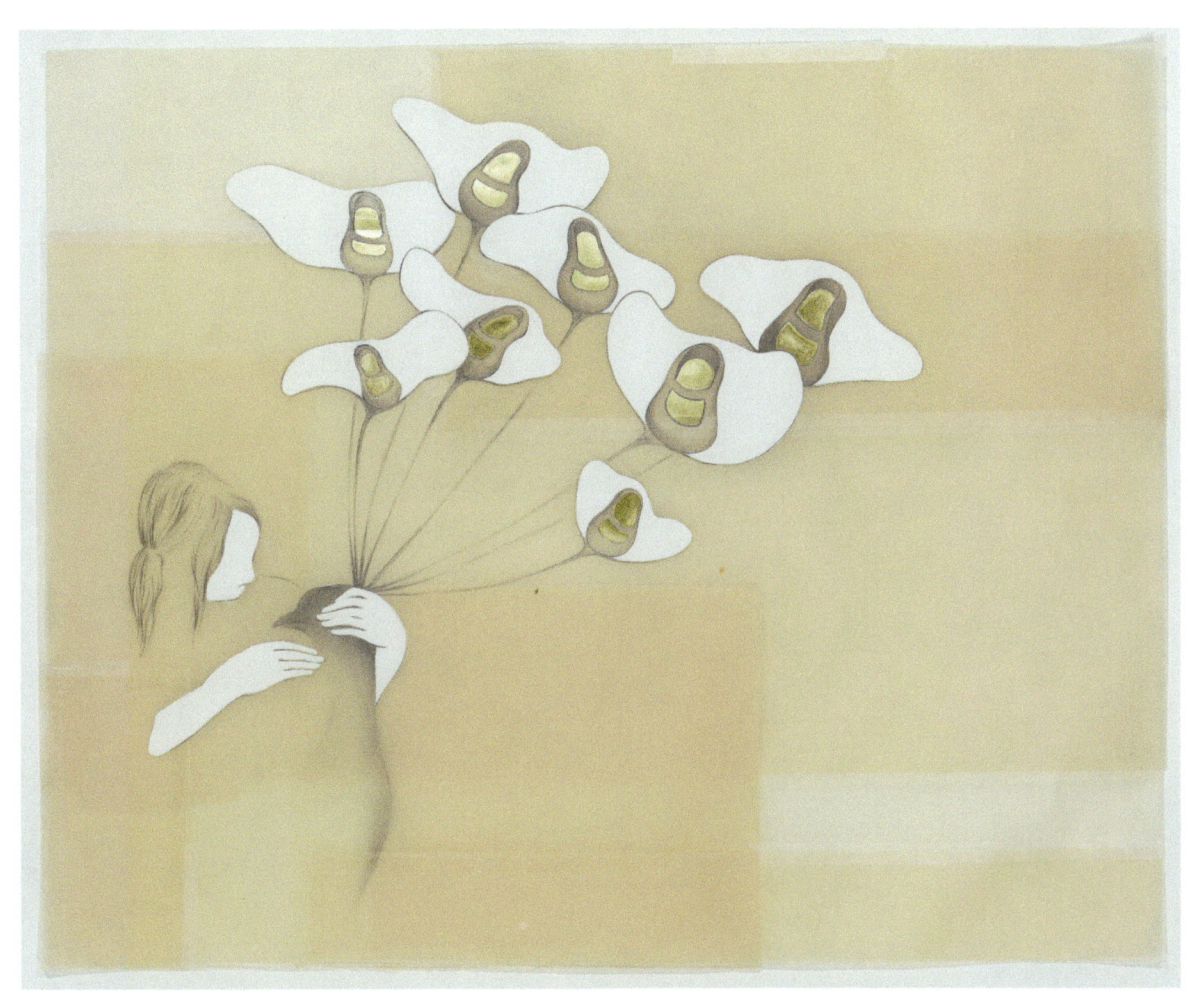

Murray's sculptural works transform images of nature into expressions of human emotions. The work is at times a cheerful take on the natural world, and at other times it possesses a sinister edge. Some of the sculptures boast a childlike, romantic innocence. Her work is an attempt to offset the inevitable assault of age, by sustaining a vision of childhood. Sensuality guides the relationship between the work and the spectator, a much more immediate contact to be established through sight. As Murray explains, she wants "the viewer's first impression to be that of children finding a new toy, desiring to touch it."

Murray brilliantly merges these competing themes in her sculpture *Unicorn*, where she creates this mystical creature by combining a horse and a narwhale. She casts a large horse skull in bronze, — which came from a police horse — and a narwhal horn into a glass mold. The light emanating from the stand, through the smoked plexiglass base and spot lights set under the upper lip of the stand, enhances the "other worldly" quality of the piece. Shadows on the skull are dramatized and the horn glows softly. As myth goes, only females pure of heart can see or attract a unicorn. However, Murray puts the "purity" of her little girls into question with *Unicorn*, since the unicorn is represented as a skull.

CAGING THE SONG BIRD
2012
leather, velvet, wood
15 x 10 x 10 in.

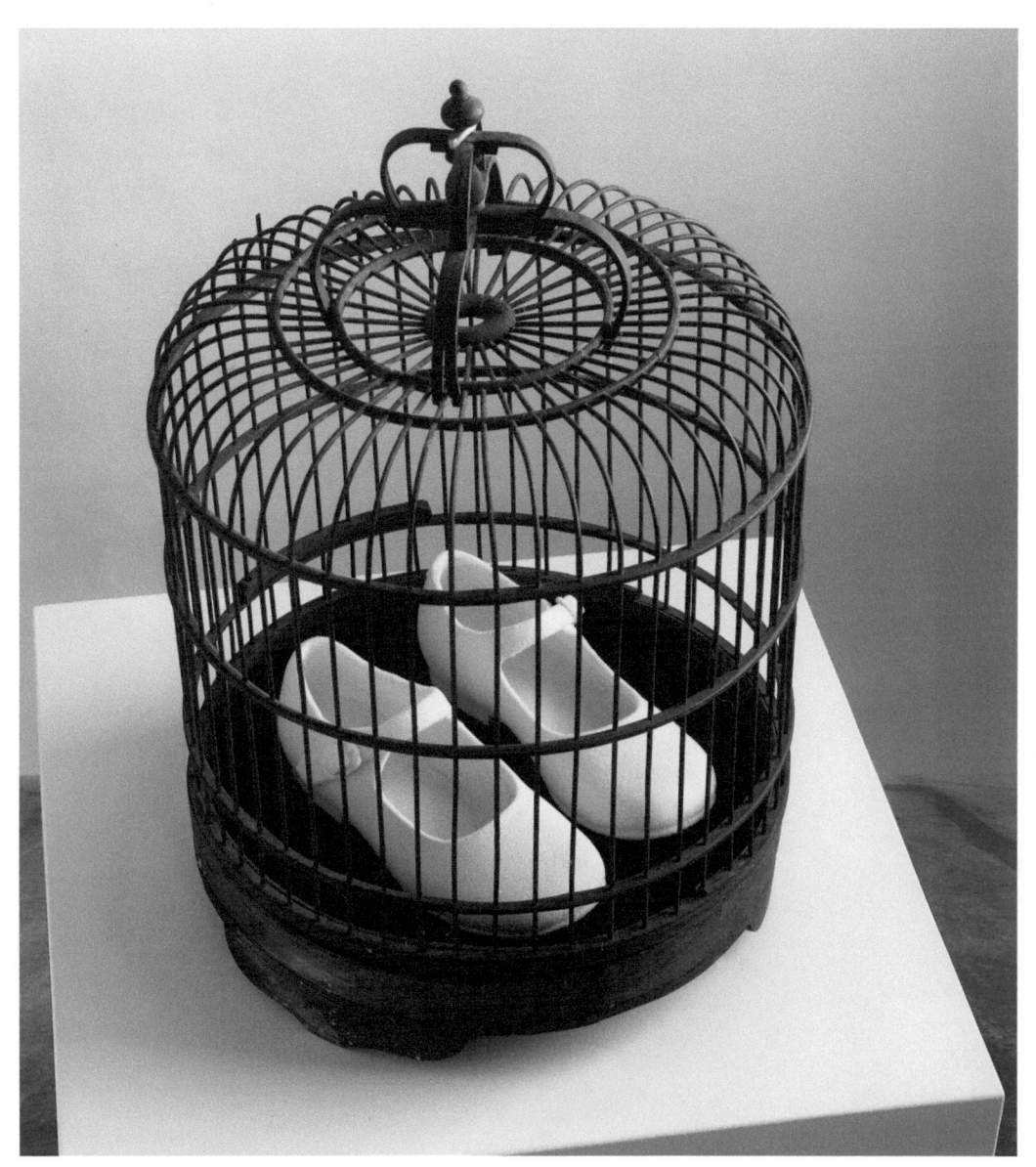

UNICORN
2011
bronze, wood, LED lights, glass
78 x 44 x 30 in.

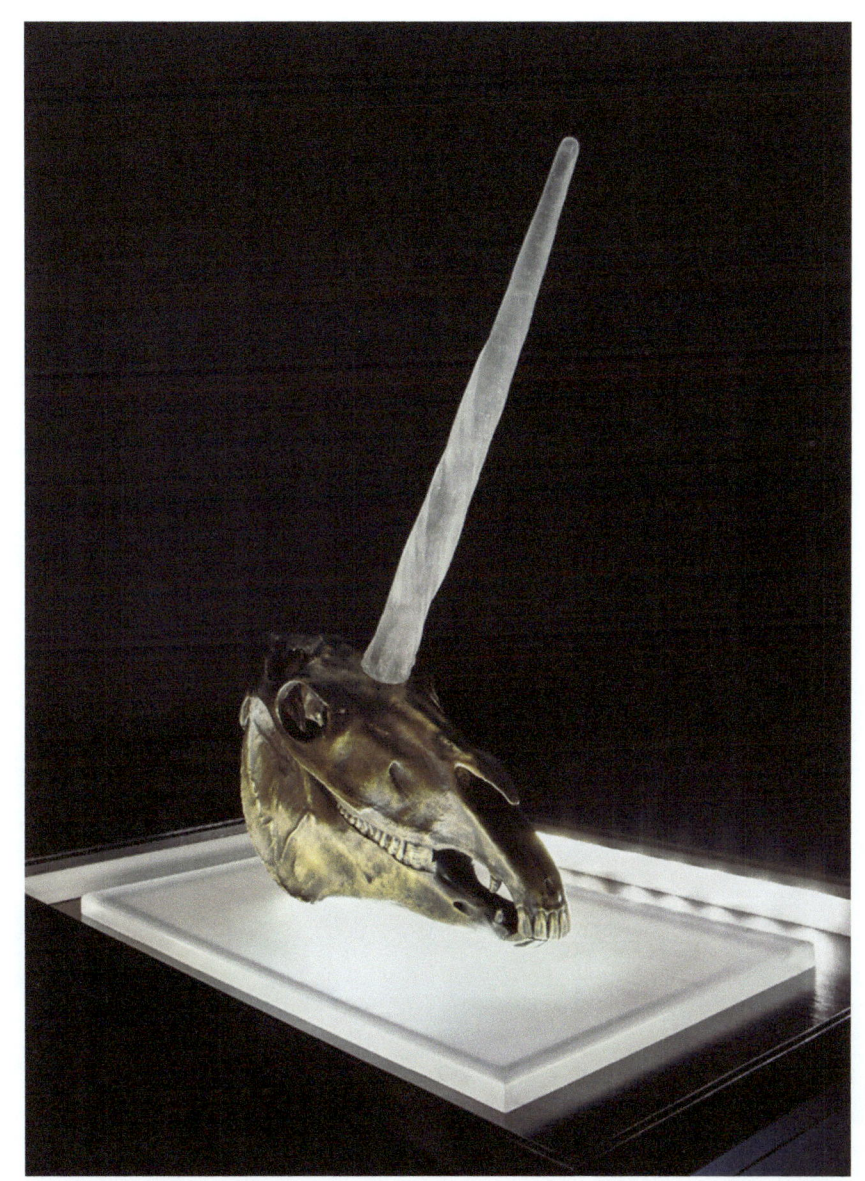

KINDLING
2012
antlers, LED lights, plexiglass, wood
46 x 31½ x 31½ in.

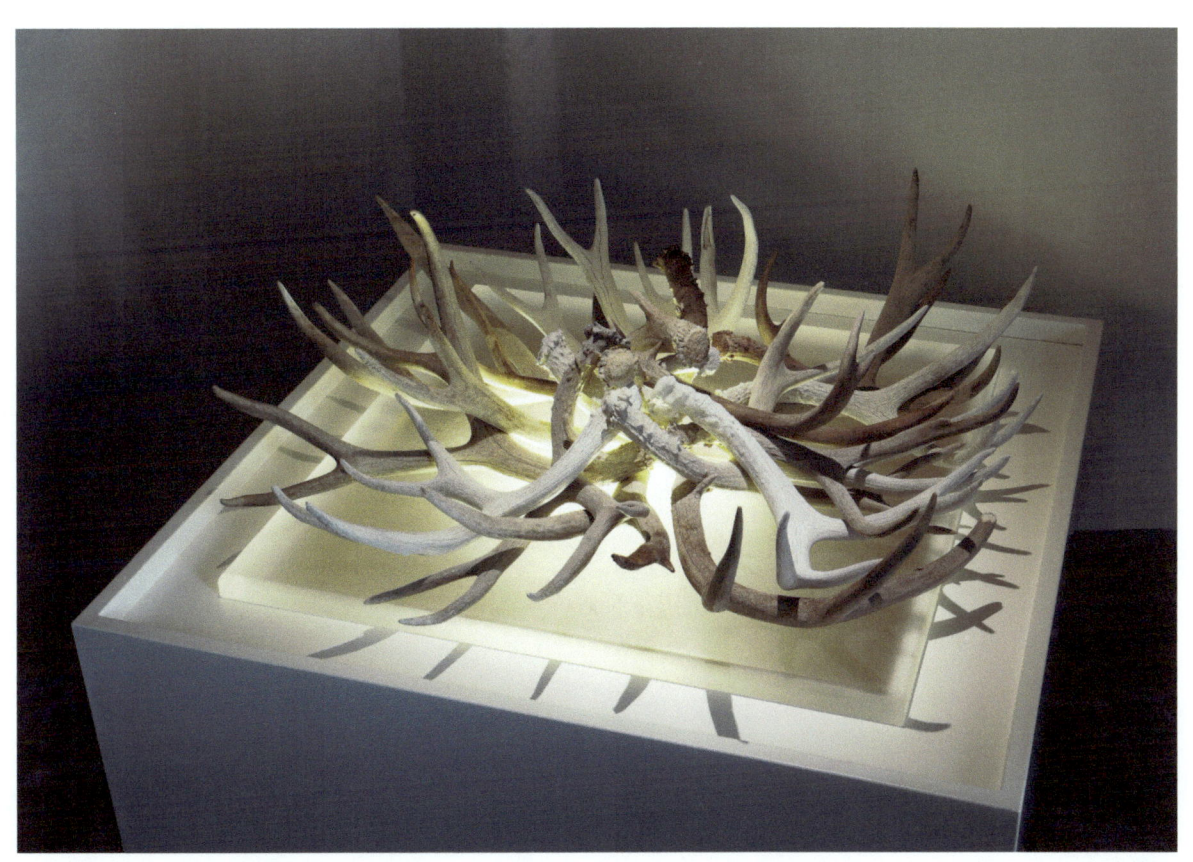

TUMBLEWEED ◆
2013
burnt antlers, paint
(variable sizes)

50

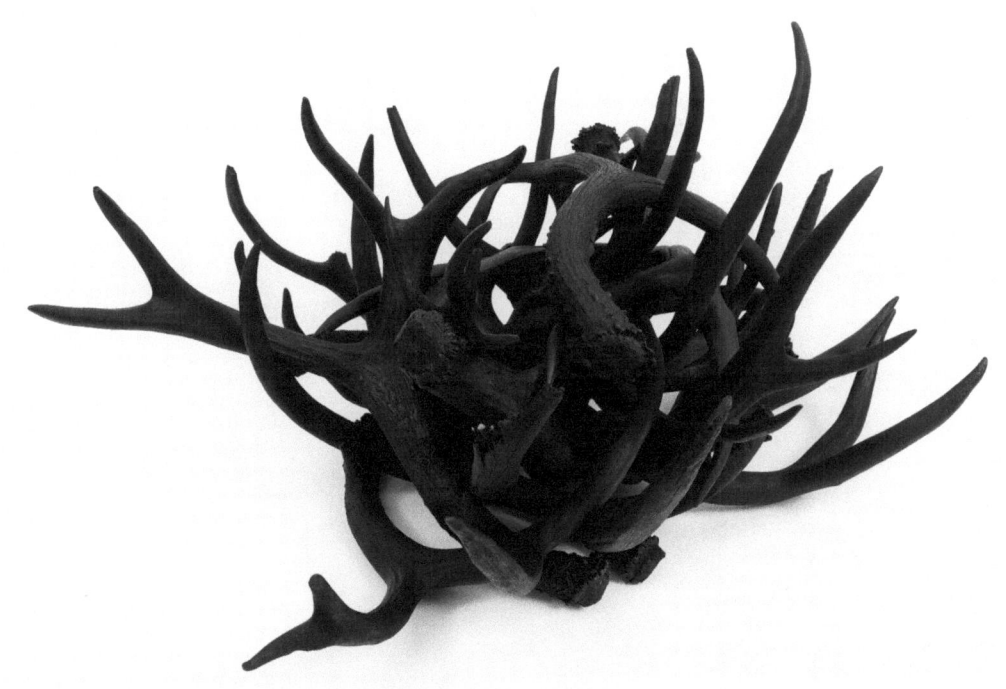

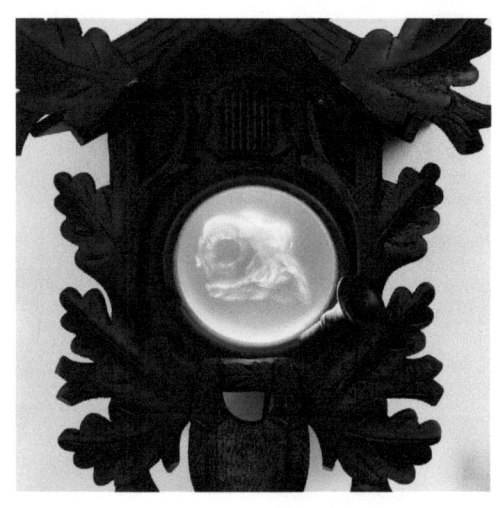

PAST PRESENT FUTURE ◆
2013
LED lights, glass, plexiglass, wood
46 x 27 x 5 in. (3 part pieces, measurements are wall coverage)

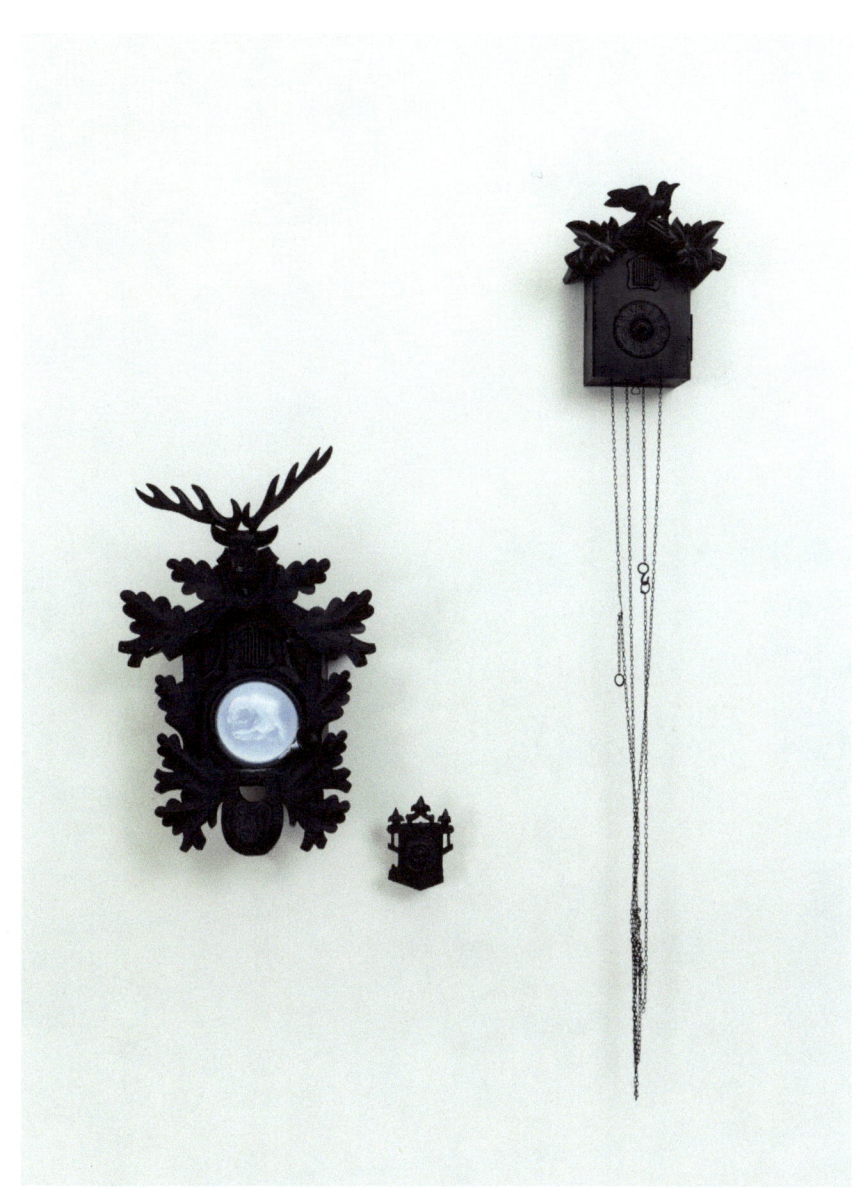

GHOST TREE #40
2013
13 x 11 x 5½ in.
led lights, glass, plexiglass, wood
2013

PENELOPE
2012
LED lights, glass, plexiglass, wood
40 x 23 x 5½ in.

HARVESTING TEARS
2013
Mirror, Antlers, Glass
6x 28 x 28 in.

ARTIST BIOGRAPHY

Born in Britain, artist Tatyana Murray is now based in New York City. Being a self-taught artist, imagination and intuition play a significant role in the development of her artistic vision. When she got off the plane, arriving in New York over 15 years ago, she was struck by what she describes as "the piercing white, blue light". This seminal moment made light a constant in Murray's work ever since — Her work is centered on light, and there is often an organic aspect to the work as well.

Murray's earlier Candy Flower series — matt, pastel colored forms — takes on a life of its own, as light changes throughout the day. The embellished beads and metallic thread in her Discarded Cardboard series sparkles like dreamy underwater scenes. And, her most recent Light Series focuses on light itself. Without light, the etched image is invisible and basically nonexistent.

Murray started showing her work in her mid 20s, and was given her first solo show in Manhattan. She has been exhibited in New York City, London, Paris, Vienna, Barcelona, Cannes, Miami, Bahamas and Venice.

SOLO EXHIBITIONS

2013   *In The Woods*, BOSI Contemporary, New York, NY
2012   *Works in Light*, Zadok Gallery, Miami, FL
2011   *Entre Phantasia et Phainesthai*, Jas Gallery, Paris
2010   Tripoli Gallery of Contemporary Art, Hamptons , NY
2009   National Arts Club, New York, NY
2006   *Morphosis*, Habres & Partner, Vienna, Austria
2004   *Drawings*, JG | Contemporary / James Graham & Sons, New York, NY
2002   *Transmutations*, JG | Contemporary, New York, NY
       Transmutations, James Graham & Sons, New York, NY
2001   *Girls Just Want to Have Fun*, Blains Gallery, London
1999   *Random Grace*, I-20 Gallery, New York, NY

GROUP EXHIBITIONS & ARTFAIRS

2013   *Illuminators*, OK Harris, "Illuminators", New York, NY
2013   *3D*, Birnam Woods Gallery, New York, NY
2011   Palais du Festival Cannes Film Festival, Cannes, France
2010   Boltax Gallery; Shelter Island, NY
       Art & Guest / Grand Palais, A. Gallery, Paris, France
       Tools for Thought, Sotheby's, New York, NY
2009   *Californication*, Showtime House - MDA Studio, New York, NY
       The Common Mind, CuetoProject, New York, NY
2007   Zoo Art Fair, BISCHOFF/WEISS, London, UK
2004   *Wood Work*, JG | Contemporary, New York, NY
       Slice and Dice, curated by Alois Kronschläger, Visual Arts Gallery, New York, NY
       Colorscapes, Cooper Classic Collection, New York, NY
2003   *Uptown / Downtown*, JG | Contemporary / James Graham & Sons, New York, NY
2002   *Concepts for New Sculpture*, Peggy Guggenheim Collection, Venice . Travelled to
       Dorotheum Gallery, Vienna; Goodwood Sculpture Park, Goodwood, UK
       ART NEWYORK, Kunstraum auf Zeit, Linz, Austria
       Art 2002, London Art Fair, London, UK
       Supranatural, Canary Wharf, London, UK

2001   Art 2001, London Art Fair, London, UK
1999   Galleria Zero, Barcelona, Spain
       Blains Fine Art, London, UK
1998   *Texture*, Vibrant Gallery, New York, NY
       4th Annual International Exhibition of Women's Art, Soho 20, curated by Leslie
       Jones, New York, NY
1997   Phoenix Gallery, curated by Laura Hoptman, New York, NY

SELECTED PRESS

2012   Annie Fabricant, "Tatyana Murray's Dystopia: A Powerful Expression of a Child's
       Nightmare, Lord of the Flies Tribalism, a Fantastical Realm and the Human
       Condition," *The Huffington Post*, October.
2011   Rhoni Blankenhorn, "Discovery series: Interview with Tatyana Murray,"
       Company, October.
       "La lumière comme medium essential," *Contemporain(s)*, March – May.
       Marc Beaulieux, "Une Visite, un corp de coeur ," *La Gazette Drout*, March.
2006   Die Presse, *Kunstmarkt*, July.
2002   "Getting right to the art of Nature," THE WHARF, January.
       Robert C. Morgan, *ARTnews*, December.
2001   "Sounds like fun," *The Independent*, May.
       "Concept for new sculpture," *Goodwood*, May.
       "Fantasy Figures," *Harpers & Queen*, April.
       "Primary Colors," *Evening Standard*, April.
       "Candy Girl," *Tatler*, April.
1999   Roberta Smith, *The New York Times*, July.
       Jenny Shears, "Fuzzy reception," *Surface Magazine*, June.

BOSI Contemporary was established by Sandro Bosi, an art dealer based in New York and London. Active in both primary and secondary markers, the gallery occupies the space at 48 Orchard Street (between Grand and Hester) and it focuses its attention on creating a dynamic space for artists and other art practioners to realize their vision and establish a platform for discourse that will nurture a thoughtful and creative community as well as attract new audiences.

International in scope, the gallery exhibits and communicates the work of both emerging and established artists, selected for their unique aesthetic language and fascinating vision. In addition, BOSI Contemporary annually organizes an exhibition dedicated to an artist of historical importance.

Published by BOSI Contemporary, on the occasion of the exhibition Tatyana Murray: *In the Woods* on view from May 5 to June 2, 2013.

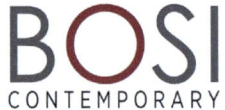

BOSI Contemporary
48 Orchard Street
New York, NY 10002
www.bosicontemporary.com